take that

· IN PRIVATE · IN PRIVATE ·

Alex Kadis
Photographs by Philip Ollerenshaw

Virgin

First published in Great Britain in 1995 by Virgin Books
an imprint of Virgin Publishing Limited
332 Ladbroke Grove London W10 5AH

ISBN: 086369 930 8

Printed and bound by Proost, Belgium.

Designed by Slatter~Anderson. For Virgin Publishing: Philip Dodd (Publisher), Carolyn Price
(Project editor). Editorial assistance from Anne Cree

To Our Fans

Well here it is, personal portraits of the five of us and a whole bunch of our favourite photographs.

We've been captured in pictures by Philip Ollerenshaw, one of our official photographers who has complete access to us on and off stage, and in words by Alex Kadis who's been writing features about us from the very beginning and knows us inside out. Of anybody we knew, we could trust them to give you the true picture of Take That.

The result is this book - down to earth and honest - with candid profiles of each of us, revealing stuff that even we didn't realize about ourselves. Some of it made us laugh, some of it we found touching.

We hope you enjoy reading it as much as we enjoyed making it.

love Howard

love Mark!

love Robbie

love Gaz xx

love, Jason xx

"We've not changed have we? Fame hasn't made us into horrible people has it? Are we doing alright do you think?" Mark Owen is a worrier. It's his nature. Is Jason's ankle any better? Is Take That's stage show still fresh and entertaining? Are the girls outside the hotel cold? Are the fans getting their money's worth? It's no accident of nature that he's the hearthrob in the group.

"He is just cute. Really cute" says Robbie. "Even his trainers are cute and not smelly like everyone else's. And you know, if he signs an autograph for a fan, he can't just put 'Love Mark', he has to say who it's to, write a little personal message: 'It was nice meeting you, hope your gran's feeling well, give my love to your mum.' **He honestly thinks that they'll love him less if he doesn't do all that.**"

Mark

he is just cute. really cute. says Robb

"Even his trainers are cute and not smell like everyone else's. And you know, if he signs an autograph for a fan, he can't just put 'Love Mark', he has to say who it's to, write a really personal message – 'it was nice meeting you, hope your gran's feeling well, give my love to your mum' – he honestly thinks they'll love him less if he doesn't do all that."

Mark has won just about every award available where looks are the criteria being judged. And Gary worries about this. "He says it doesn't bother him but it does. I worry about little Marky, it's a lot of responsibility."

For someone who's worry quota is so high, Mark Owen is a remarkably chipper chap. He has an endearing habit of talking to himself. He's often to be found wandering aimlessly, babbling away quite happily to no one in particular. He sometimes goes into hyperdrive – especially if he's had a glass of red wine – he has no tolerance of alcohol whatsoever! And yet, the others in Take That have a quiet respect for him which is rarely spoken.

Says Gary, "Marky has such good taste, you know, and he never boasts about what he's bought either. He'll turn up with a nice little car and you'll say: 'Oh that's nice Marky.' And he'll say: 'Oh I've had it for about six months now.' "

Mark rarely loses his temper. But the night the video crew polished the stage in Berlin during the Euro tour of '94, Mark stormed off stage and screamed at Skippy the stage manager. "What the hell do you think you're doing letting them polish our stage?"

"I apologized straight away. I thought, hold on, this isn't me, I must be tired."

When Mark has had enough he likes to be alone. Upon his return to London after that tour, he went for a walk on his own, without security saying: "I'm sick of being followed everywhere, I want to be on my own."

"He likes his own company, does Mark, I admire that in a person," says Gary.

Mark is a real animal lover – at his mum and dad's house

One night, at a gig in Copenhagen, a girl flings her childhood Snoopy toy onto the stage. It is addressed to Mark. Attached to it are pictures of the little girl growing up with the toy. It's been with her all her life.

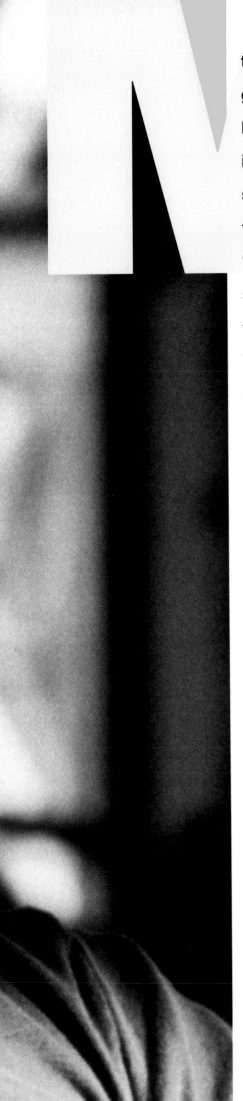

there is a budgie, a dog, a goldfish and a hamster. Now he lives with his pet iguana, Nirvana, and he's a soft touch for a hungry cat, too.

"Where I live there are a lot of stray cats. At the moment I'm feeding about six of them!" You would think, being Britain's and just about everywhere else's sexiest man, Mark would be full of sickening confidence. Charmingly, he isn't. He is least confident about his singing.

"One night on stage I could feel my voice going half-way through the show. I was so fed up I nearly cried. I'm not very confident about my singing anyway. When we had a month off last year I went and booked myself some singing lessons. I didn't have time to start from scratch so the woman said bring in some of your favourite records and sing to

them. So that's what I did. I'd put a record on and sing and she'd tell me where I was going wrong."

One memorable night, at a gig in Copenhagen, a girl flings her childhood Snoopy toy onto the stage. It is addressed to Mark. Attached to it are pictures of the little girl growing up with the toy. It's been with her all her life. The next day Mark writes the girl a letter saying that although he loves the Snoopy, she has had so much history with it that he can't possibly keep it. In his letter he explains that as he is on tour he doesn't have a box handy but he'll keep the Snoopy dog until he gets home and then he'll post it back to her. He keeps to his word.

"That's the one! That's the shop! Oh yes, Barlow can smell it now! There's a bargain in there." Gary is leaning out of the car window like a man possessed. There is only one thing he's as passionate about as he is about songwriting and that's shopping! But if you embarrass easily, don't accompany him on one of his sprees. Inside the shop of his desires, in Copenhagen's antique district, he fingers a small, silver cigarette box. He has just been told the price.

"*How* much?! Oh I don't think I can afford that."

The snooty woman behind the counter looks over her half-moon specs at the scruffy anoraked character before her as if to say: "Hm, I thought as much!"

Gary slowly smirks, takes a deep breath and whispers,

"Right this is where the embarrassing bit starts."

Gary

He looks the woman straight in the eye and says: "Well now, I know what the *shop* price is but what are you going to sell it to *me* for?"

"Oh no sir, the price is not negotiable."

How wrong she is, for little does she know she is face to face with **Bargain Barlow, expert shopper and renowned bargain hunter!** He is obsessed with home improvement and the one thing that got him through the miserable Euro tour of 1994 was his planned visit to Harvey Nichols when he returned to London.

"There are two things I'm looking forward to, buying a bed in Harvey Nichs and getting a dog. I want a German Shepherd. I'd like one from a rescue foundation – one that really needs a good home. I can't wait. But it'll be a guard dog, I think, an outside dog." True to his word he found Jess later that month.

Gary knows what he likes and his pleasures are simple ones. Croissants in the morning, coffee on the boil all day, Cadbury's Dairy Milk, and peace and quiet.

Gary is very confident about his songwriting, especially after meeting Elton John.

"He told me I had a talent and if I wanted to I could make a career out of songwriting for life. I had never thought about it before. From that day on my life changed."

He's not all confidence, though. He does worry about his weight.

"I can't tell you what I was eating during our month off last year – it would make you ill. One day I looked down and saw my gut. So I phoned Jason and I said, right, let's do a diet.

The pinnacle of Gary's career – indeed his life so far has

been to win two Ivor Novello awards.

"For me that was recognition for everything I've tried to achieve. I was made up. "

Music is Gary's life. In his spare time he will write songs. One night, he finds a beautiful grand piano in a hotel restaurant and sits down to play 'Yesterday's Girl', a song intended for the next Take That album. He next plays a song he has written for his mum. He was in the loft a while ago and found some pictures of her when she was younger which inspired him.

"I haven't played this to my mum yet. I want her to get a surprise when it's on an album."

A middle-aged couple stop by and look on, they have no idea who this person is but they are enchanted by his music.

Apart from controlling his

"Sorry girls, it's only **me,** the others **haven't come."**

weight, Gary doesn't care much about the way he looks. In fact, he quite enjoys his anti-hero status. He recalls a time when a maid took photographs of his hotel room and was caught before she managed to sell the pictures to the tabloids.

"Can you imagine the shame?" he winces, "Gary Barlow middle-aged man with seventeen copies of *Homes and Gardens* by the bed and a pipe and slippers!"

When he turns up at a restaurant without the other members of the group he apologizes to the convoy of fans who have followed him there.

"Sorry girls, it's only me, the others haven't come." Then aside: "I expect they'll all want to go home now they know the others aren't here! I reckon half the time we meet and greet fans they leave and they think, who was that scruffy bastard hanging round Take That!"

" *The one thing I*

never realized when I

first joined **Take**

That *was that*

I would meet four

of **the best**

friends *I would*

ever *have* **"**

Gary

Robbie

When Nirvana's front man Kurt Cobain died, Robbie was in Copenhagen. He silently took himself off to a quiet location to do some thinking. He was depressed. He sat on the flat roof of the hotel smoking. It was like a fridge out there but he didn't seem to notice.

"He's leaving a daughter behind. . . "

Robbie's pop star persona isn't actually too far removed from his real personality: **He *is* a scream, he *does* always have something to say for himself, he *is* that cheeky, cheery chap** from Stoke that you see on television. The only problem with personas is that they only tell half the story. And Robbie Williams is a real dichotomy.

" You see, I like being funny "

Robbie is outspoken, funny, loud and protective over those he loves. The son of a stand-up comedian and a florist, he can crack a good joke and make you up a nice bouquet. "I used to work in the flower shop, actually. I can do a £12.50 bouquet – a bit of gypsophila, a bit of green, and then your sprays. And I can do a nice ribbon for it too." The only thing he couldn't handle in the shop was the money.

"I can't add up or subtract. I'm dyslexic. I'm bad with numbers and I get my b's, d's and 9's round the wrong way. I was a grade A student at school in the first and second year and then they put me into a middle class. It was very embarrassing."

He's still not good with money now. When he had none to spend he didn't much care, now he's financially comfortable, he doesn't quite **know what to do with it all.**

"I don't feel any different now I've got money to be honest. I still don't really spend. I bet I spend less than you do. I bet I spend less than all the others in the group."

Robbie feels better about looking in the mirror now he's lost weight.

"I avoid all dairy produce and white bread. I eat tuna and lots of chicken. Sometimes when I'm at home I eat a whole chicken in a day. Just cold with a bit of salt on the side. There's hardly any fat on it, it's good protein and it builds muscle tissue. So instead of going to the gym, I eat a chicken!"

His latest trick to get people to see how lean and muscly he is, is this: He pokes tentatively at a rib and says: "Ooh, I

think I've broken a rib. Have a feel for me."

So you feel about and find the painful part isn't a rib at all but a muscle. So he says, all innocence: **"Oh a muscle? Not another muscle!"**

Robbie relies on his own sense of humour for entertainment.

"Sometimes if I haven't been very funny in an interview I get fed up. You see, I like being funny. When I read the interviews back afterwards I make myself laugh!"

It's the other side to his character that many fans would find surprising. The other Robbie is the one who worries about his looks, who is concerned that he may have upset you – if he sees someone is down he'll say: "It's nothing I've done is it?" And he needs to be liked. And loved.

"Since I've become famous I think it's more important for me to feel liked. You'd think it would be less, but I want to be sure that people still like **me**. "

He worries about fame changing him and is constantly asking if he's big-headed yet – he knows he's easily influenced but he's not stupid.

"I don't think I've changed but, you know, it might happen and I might not know. I have to rely on people to tell me the truth."

This most stridently heterosexual of men is very protective of his gay friends and is also very physically affectionate towards all women and men regardless of their sexuality.

"I go out with Mark, our make-up guy a lot – he's gay. So what if we go to gay clubs? I'll hold his hand going down the street if I want to. I'm just naturally affectionate. I always kiss the other lads in Take That hello and goodbye – no tongues though!"

Last year Jason took his first proper holiday for ages and chose to take it alone. He packed a bag, his guitar, four books on self-discovery and some travellers cheques. For two weeks he hardly spoke to a soul. Most of the day was spent sitting on a secluded little rock he'd found, out of view of everyone, practising his guitar and soaking up the sun. Some evenings were spent taking his meals on his balcony, reading and trying to find himself. Believe it or not, he had a whale of a time.

But then, Jason is accustomed to being alone. He lives by himself in a small, modest flat and when he's at home in Manchester he often eats out alone, just him, a curry, a glass of red wine and a good book.

"I like it most of the time. **But sometimes, you know, it does get lonely."**

Although Jason's a bit of bookworm now, during his school years he avoided books like the plague. Consequently, he didn't get much of an education.

"I didn't bother much with school. I was just on automatic pilot. I took a few exams but I missed most of them. The ones I took I didn't get. Perhaps when all this is over I'll go to college. . . Although I am educating myself now really."

One of the things he has learned, he says, through being in Take That, is to handle explosive situations more carefully.

"I used to scream and shout and it wouldn't do any good so now I just stay calm. We're sane, we're adults, we can rise above all the bitching that goes on in the music industry."

Jason's new found self-control is a feature that crops up again and again. He decided some time ago to teach himself to play guitar. Since then, he's rarely seen without one in his hand. Any spare moment is spent practising. Says Mark: **"I love to watch Jason playing his guitar, his face is pure concentration."**

And then there's his eating habits. No fat, no dairy produce, no artificial sugars – except, of course, when he's scoffing his beloved curries!

When he goes on tour he takes a small black briefcase in which he carries some mind-expanding reading material and some seeds – poppy, sesame and sunflower – which he sprinkles on his sugar-free muesli doused with mineral water in the mornings. Extremely unappetizing.

"I just can't bare the thought of filling my body with crap."

But he has, it would seem, been overly abstemious in the past. A visiting physiotherapist told him straight.

"He said I was prone to injury because my diet was insufficient. I need more sugar, salt and caffeine to give me

energy. I did have very low blood pressure because of my diet. . . "

On one particular occasion, Mark was so concerned about Jason's complete lack of energy that he forced him to eat some chocolate before he went on stage.

Jason has a very fierce sense of fair play. He gets upset when Take That are separated from their musicians at social occasions – he feels their equality should be emphasized. It is he who insists that the musicians share the group's private jet to travel from country to country. Although the others groan when he "gets on a whinge" they also respect him for it.

"Jason won't have a bad word to say about anyone no matter how much they've pissed him off," says Rob, "he refuses to gossip or do people down and I really admire that."

"What right have I to judge anyone?" is Jason's reasoning.

He says he leads as normal a life as possible given his circumstances. He still insists on going shopping about town without a bodyguard, his only safety precautions being a woolly hat and a pair of clear glasses which he thinks are a disguise. Useless.

Gary is Jason's closest friend in the group and in true best mate fashion he has this to say:

"I pity the girl who ends up with **him**. Who would put up with **that**?"

Gary's mum, on the other hand, thinks Jason's pretty wonderful.

"They're all lovely lads, but I think apart from Gary, Jason is my favourite. He seems to be very fond of his mother. He really is a lovely lad."

" *The more*

famous *we*

get the **more** *us*

five stick together.

We *love* *each*

other. I'd **die** *for the*

guys in this group"

"I wasn't being unfriendly earlier on when you were all at the café and I was sitting on my own. I was trying to write. I don't want you to think I was being funny."

Howard Donald is a mystery. He's the member of Take That who reveals least about himself. He's genuinely shy and there isn't a pretentious bone in his body. He has, it would appear, been almost completely **untouched by his fast-moving, powerful and lucrative career.**

"God this is strange isn't it?" he ponders. "I never thought we'd be this famous or that I would have money.

" I never thought we'd be this famous"

I remember in the early days I was walking down the street with Nigel, our manager, and I saw this car I liked. I said: 'Oh look at that car, Nigel.' And he said: 'You'll be able to buy one of those one day.' But I never really believed it."

Howard likes his hair. Before the dreads he only washed it once a week now he never washes it – the others call him a "soap dodger." While we're on the subject you might as well know that he never uses soap on his armpits because he thinks it makes you sweat more.

Jason is a big fan of Howard's sense of humour. "He's just so deadpan-he cracks me up." On the tour bus one day, Jason and Mark are discussing animal cruelty with regards to horse racing. Jason says that he thinks the horses enjoy the race and uses the

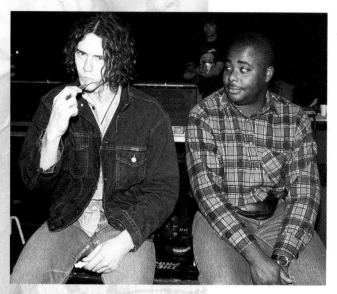 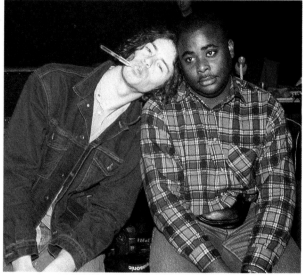

example of the time when Desert Orchid strutted onto the track and reared up on his hind legs to show off his beauty to the crowd. Mark disagrees and says that using any animal for sport is cruel. Howard hasn't said

a word and then innocently says: "But it's OK to kill birds and cats though innit?" Of course he doesn't mean it, but it's enough to make Jason and Mark cry with laughter.

Human suffering of any sort profoundly upsets Howard.

An early story from Nigel concerns a time when Take That went to a hospice to visit patients who were dying from AIDS-related diseases.

"Howard was introduced to a gay man who was thin and dying from AIDS and he just put his arms round him and burst into tears. I was deeply touched by it."

Bearing this in mind you can believe the sort of things that go through Howard's mind sometimes when he is on stage.

"One night, I don't know why I started thinking it, but I was on the stage and I wondered if any of the girls out there had lost their parents. I know it's a strange thing to think but they all had such sad faces and I wondered how they would cope being without their parents at such a young age. It made me really sad. Maybe it's because I think about it all the time. I'm so worried about being without my mum and dad."

This sometime preoccupation with death also spills over into Howard's "hobbies". He is fascinated by anything gruesome.

"Look, I'm not sick! I don't watch Vietnam videos for kicks you know, it does genuinely upset me. But it also fascinates me."

This morbid fascination runs into books, videos and films about various subjects of gore. His latest acquisition is a set of three videos called *The Faces of Death.*

"It's all the stuff they can't put on the news. It's very upsetting, especially the animal bits – it's enough to make you vegetarian. I had to watch it in stages at first but I'm. . . what's the word. . . curious."

A special thank you to:

Soozii, Ying, James, Paul, Barry, Gus, Jenny, Skippy and the crew, Sean and Lou, Phil, Carolyn and Mal at Virgin. Sheila, Christalla and Maria Kadis, Louise Kent, The TT Mums, Tim Suter at the BBC, Simon Kenton and everyone at Idols, Philip's Mum and above all to Howard, Mark, Gary, Jason, Rob and Nigel Martin-Smith for making it all possible.

We thank you all.

Alex Kadis
Philip Ollerenshaw

Available on video:

Take That & Party,
Take That Live at Wembley,
Everything Changes,
Berlin